A Collection of Spoken Word

Authored By
OneNess Sankara

Word-Sound Volume 1
A Collection of Spoken Word

Copyright © 2015 by OneNess Sankara

All rights reserved. No part of this publication may be reproduced, distributed, or transmitted in any form or by any means, including photocopying, recording, or other electronic or mechanical methods, without the prior written permission of the publisher, except in the case of brief quotations embodied in critical reviews and certain other non-commercial uses permitted by copyright law.

ISBN 978-0-9932728-0-6

Sankara House Publications
First Edition

Illustrator: Carmelle Powell of Pfe Freedom Arts
Designer: Jeremy Salmon of WeDesign.media

Many thanks to proofreaders:
Daniella Blechner and Lana Homeri

Content

Preface	Page 7
Release me	Page 9
Introduction	Page 11

Word-Sounds:

Today	Page 12
Brotha	Page 14
3monkeys	Page 16
Colours	Page 18
No Womban	Page 20
Hair peace	Page 22
Home	Page 25
Unrested Souls	Page 26
Be	Page 28
A Womban's Journey	Page 31
Endnotes	Page 35
Biography	Page 37

Word Sound Volume 1 A Collection of Spoken Word

Acknowledgements

Asante Sana. Thank you to loved ones for your support on this journey. Thanks Mumsy Georgina for nurturing the word and thank you Pops Ashton for passing on the gift of sound.

Thanks to my iron sharpeners: BKS Collective and my spirit fam: Flow PD. Thanks to those of you who are reading and energising this work.

Livication

The book is livicated to the Soul that was known as Ethan Nedd-Bruce. Your life taught me so many lessons. It was always my intention to livicate this book to you; however I had no idea that I would be calling you an ancestor.

Rest well in your celestial works, Prince.

Love Always

Aunty One

Word Sound Volume 1 A Collection of Spoken Word

Preface[1]

"I don't want realism. I want Magic" *Tennessee Williams*

As a purpose mentor and quantum creative, epic journeys have become embedded in the fabric of existence. A magical mystical aspect of my alchemical abundance is the gift of poetry. Poetry has shown me the wonders of the world though word and sound. Poetry has guided me and chided me. It has shown me the truth of being made in the image and likeness of the Creator. Words have shown themselves to me through many forms and though my ego would have me believe that this was my very own Sankara super power-it is in fact a power that is accessible to us ALL. It is the power of the word. It is the power of the word through sound; vibration. It is the power to create and transform worlds.

Definition of a Poet

Being gifted with the passion and ability to write and perform is a true blessing; so much so that I feel as though I was born to be a lover of words: a conduit of sound.

The great master poet, Gil Scott Heron[2], defined a poet as, "Someone who uses words to communicate more than just ordinary conversation"[3]. By his definition I have been a poet since I was about three years old. I 'wrote' my first poem somewhere around 1988. Since then, I continued to write. I wrote for varying reasons. I wrote because teachers and elders told me to...I wrote because my friends and family enjoyed my words and, most of all, I wrote because my spirit had gifted me with beautiful words. I always 'wrote' in my head first...That's where it consciously starts for me. I always hear the word-sound first. Then I put pen to paper as a means of recording. Recording for what? For a long time I didn't know. However, I continued to engage with this process of; put pen to paper, paper on shelf, press repeat. I went on like this for many years until I found the world of performance poetry and great artists such as Zena Edwards, Talaam Acey and Mutabaruka to name a

few.
History. Herstory. Mystory

Running parallel and integral to my journey as a poet has always been my journey into spiritual growth and cultural awareness.
At the age of 21, my life dramatically changed and words were right there waiting to receive me, to guide and show me the way. Poetry led me to history. My history. Hundreds of thousands of years of history. History that belonged to me. And it is through that history that I found many blessings. One of which was the Griot. The Griot is, in simple terms, (though the Griot is far from 'simple') a master of the oratory arts whose role includes delivering history as a poet, praise singer, and wandering musician.

The Spoken Word

"The Griot is a repository of oral tradition"[4]. The Griot was also said to have great knowledge of the sacred power of sound. This idea resonated deeply within as I already had an instinct about oral traditions. An instinct that was contrary to what I had been taught through my mainstream education. An education that had placed an emphasis on the written word. If it wasn't in a library then it wasn't worth the paper that it wasn't written on- was the underlying message. This attitude connoted an inferiority of the oral transmission of information. It implied an uneducated assumption that our ancestors, who placed emphasis on word-sound, did so out of ignorance and a lack of knowledge of the written text. This couldn't be farther from the truth as our oratory ancestors have displayed. From the mysteries of the Nile Valley to the high science of the Dogon peoples, oral tradition has played a fundamental role.

So where does that leave a contemporary Wordologist? It leaves them somewhere between the page and the stage creating new mediums while respecting, learning, and drawing from the rich foundations that our ancestors have laid.
Ashe (And so it is.)

Release me

(This poem welcomes being read aloud[5])

Release me Release me
No more bondage of captivity
Take me out of your head and put me in your mouth
Take me into your vibrational space and let me out
Release me fast Release me slow
Release me smooth or staccato
Release me with base or vibrato just let me live
I was birthed to give but still waiting to take form
Release me from being still born

Release me from my rage, from the cage of this page
let me take my place on your life's stage
gloat with me, quote with me, gargle in your throat with me
use me, adapt me, affirm me, rap me,
sing me, clap me, do anything but trap me

For I was born to dance on your dinner tables
Tear off your sticky labels
Give you truth disguised as fables
And tap into your inner cables

I manifest in the shaman, the layman, the mistress & maiden
I am your future manifestation of history in the making
I am your instant messenger to the spirits of nature
I can be your destroyer or I can be your saviour
For I am the word and God was me
So if you truly love me, set me free.

Word Sound Volume 1 A Collection of Spoken Word

Word Sound Volume 1 A Collection of Spoken Word

Introduction

During the process of birthing Word Sound Vol 1, I was asked if I was writing a book of poetry. I found myself making the distinction that I was in fact writing a book of spoken word poetry. This led me to question why this distinction was so important to me. The answer is performance. My desire was to create a collection which could be performed. This by no means suggests that this work should not be read. On the contrary; this text was born to live diversely. Like a play. Just as one would read a play, watch a play and/ or perform a play; so could one watch, read and/or perform the writing in Word Sound Vol 1. My desire is to further a cultural expansion of how we view spoken word whilst responding to the challenge of documenting art forms that are oral in its practice and tradition.

Today[6]

Both micro and macro we hold notions of what is right and wrong. Firmly committed to fixed spaces of what is real and unreal. Our view is none but our perception. Remember- the world was once flat..... apparently!

This is what I'm doing for today
There's always today
That's why I'm living for today
Buzzing in my own creative way
Don't care what they say
That's why I'm living my way today
See, at this point tomorrow isn't guaranteed
It's all about now so forget what you believe
I give my middle finger so society better believe it
It's all about my life so I am going to use it
I'm going to use immediately, creatively
Don't care what I see today it's all about me
Today I'm gonna skin my teeth walk down the street
Light on my feet don't care who I meet
Today I'm choosing me
Nobody's gonna use me, abuse me
Or try to confuse me
I'm going with my own agenda
A born pretender, today I don't have a fiver to lend ya
Today I'm gonna be like cha, you can't borrow my car
Don't care, forget who you are
For so long it's been all about you
You, you, you, your issues so now hear the coup
I'm more than just a name, number or a file
A cute face and a smile
Forget the big picture my life is worthwhile
My life's worth more than a grave in a park
I wanna make my mark
My existence recognised as art

Word Sound Volume 1 A Collection of Spoken Word

I want my opinions heard, a final word
Acknowledgement of what my life was worth
You see, it's all too late for me
So don't be fooled by what you see
Look into my eyes they no longer gleam
All I have is the dream of what could have been
You see dear death has taken me
I no longer have a reality
I no longer have my life to waste
I can no longer touch smell feel or taste
I cannot live for the moment for the moment has gone
I no longer have a say yet the world still going on
And as the world still turns
I wish that I learned way before now what my life was worth
I hope when you wake from this dream you remember
Race, creed, colour or gender
Giver, taker, receiver or sender you are life in all its splendour
You may not even remember this night
But just for me remember one thing
Love your life

Brotha

In 2007, we lost a great brotha. Reggie Pedro[7]. My community called upon me to create word sound for this brotha. This is for you Brotha. Rest in Beauty My Brotha

"Black Brotha, Strong Brotha, there is no one above ya
I want you to know that I'm here for you forever true"[8]

No good Brother,
Wotless Brother
Unreliable Brother
And violent Brother
Apathetic Brother
Lazy Brother
Make our great ancestors roll over in their graves and disown this Brother kind of Brother
Tends to be the focus of our attention
And with blind intentions we affirm these ideas
Internalise them over years and neglect to mention & celebrate

The blessed Brotha
The strong Brotha
The kind Brotha
The loving Brotha
The great legacy continuing Brotha
The Brotha that you can bring home to your mother kind of Brotha
The Brotha that makes your sistas ask if he's got another Brotha kind of Brotha

Word Sound Volume 1 A Collection of Spoken Word

The Brotha that represents the pride in our Brothas

We must remember to love cherish nurture and
support these Brothas
For this piece was inspired by one of these Brothas
A Brotha who reminded me of the greatness in our
Brothers
RIP Brotha

3 Monkeys

She came out of the 60s. Malcolm her uncle, Nkrumah her daddy, Rosa her baby-sitter and Amy Jaques was her elder matriarch. She danced with grace, hope and vigour through Black Power and Independence yet found herself disillusioned. Feet firm in dependence. With no more bite in her bark she takes one more leap and lands on vision. Her very own vision. Vision now crushed and buried it does not rest in peace. It will not rest in peace. It wanders. It haunts.

They wanna know their name
They wanna know their crime
They want to know their purpose
Why they've returned this time

I see them on the corner
They look at me with a piercing stare
A scary air of familiarity
They see me
I cross to the other side
Coming from the other side
Lack of pride clouds the mission
The vision
My indecision of should I return

Burn Babylon/ooh I go there
I am weak I am tired.
I have retired
Illusion has replaced my fire
Coz I and I would rather live this lie
Than to consciously watch my future die
She grabbed my face and made me look her in the eye
She wanted to know, they all wanted to know, why?

They call themselves lost children
Keep knocking at my door
They know me but I don't know them

But they know that they've been here before

They know that I hear them and I do
I hear them, I hear their cries
In the dead of the night
But I don't know how they know
And they don't know how much they show their vulnerability
See it's not their guns that scare me
It's not their foul tongues that tear my soul
It's the lack of beholding a vision
"How come you hear us cry?" they say

I am a lot older than yesterday
And when sick and twisted games we play
I still see,
All I see is children branded
Name branded
And I can stand it
Gucci and Nike with Louis Vuitton in my periphery
My core is shaken evoking sankofa memories
Full HD memories of satanic plantations branding their enslaved
Surround sound I hear screams
Hot metal against raw skin
I know they are in pain
And I am the same
Branded with failure and shame
I know why they came
I can't tell them their name
I can't look them in the eyes
I can't answer their whys
I can't lead them to the light
I can't strengthen their fight

So I pump up the volume of my iPhone
or drive my coupe to avoiding stares on the way home
Take comfort & escape in a glass of fragrant merlot
And make the best lamenting liberty that had died long ago

Word Sound Volume 1 A Collection of...

Colours

Setting: London 90s
This piece in particular is written for all of society. Colours is a long hard high-pitched, bass filled scream. It is the cry for salvation. The warning of death. Is this a true story? It's a real story.

See I lay down in a room of four different colours
Up to one, two, three, four different brothers
See I was never mothered
So I never bothered
To adorn myself in clothing that covered
See the less I wore, the less I suffered for loneliness
So I rolled the herb,
Where I would send skunk smoke signals of distress
Where man dem would try to touch my breast
I remember his red gold and green string vest
Funny back then we never used words such as 'Ho' or 'Sket'
It was 'Slosher' and dutty gal.
Dat would suffice,
I know there were more but I forget
What? Do I regret going to that yard at that time?
Should I have gone at quarter to nine?

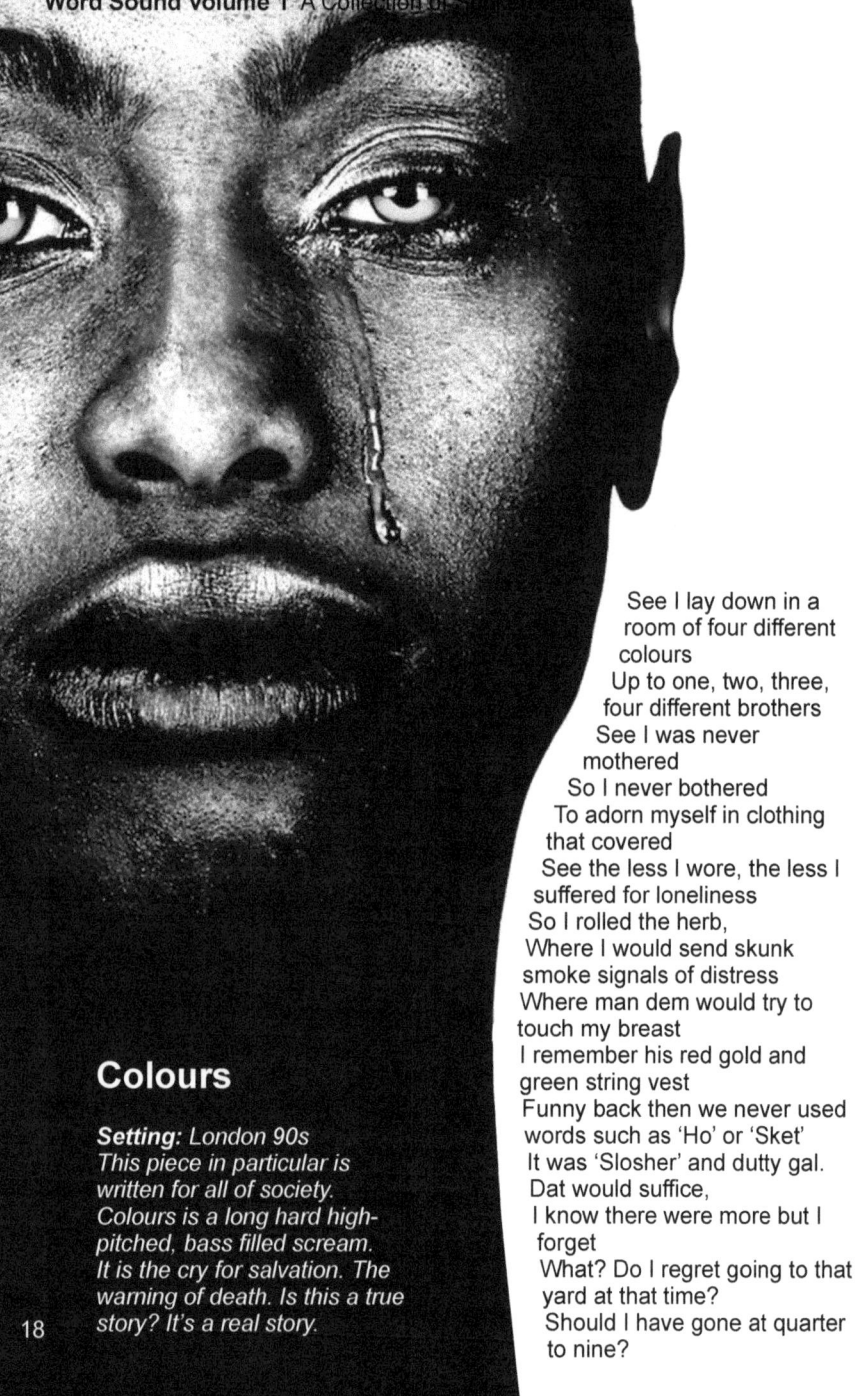

Would there have been something different on their minds?
Would they have committed a different crime?
And would I have been just fine?
Or did our problems begin from way further down the line?
So should I take back? All the way back to the middle passage?
And describe how our ancestors were debased sold and damaged?
Or do I start from when I came to England? This god forsaken country
Wandering around the streets paved with shit and being called "wogs" and "monkeys"
Or do I talk about motherless fathers and fatherless mothers?
Or the lack of support from extended family and others
Do I blame myself or do I blame those brothers?
Or do I blame the fact that there was no food in my F*ing cupboard?
Or do I even care with my heart filled with fear
As I wished and I prayed that I'd get out of there
But you see the Black God couldn't hear
And the White God didn't care
While a gruff voice said, "Don't be greedy, you've got to share"
As this beast had the nerve to stroke my hair as if he cared
And whisper in my ear, "Don't be scared"
So can someone please tell me? Why am I in hell?
And who exactly am I supposed to tell?
About these colours, these sounds and these smells
Like the devil (to me)
Yellow. I've always liked yellow, yellow is irie
You know they say my sister is yellow, well yellowish brown skinned
Brown skin you know I ……Brown skin you know I.. I I I
Hate your brown skin, and your string vest and your hat and your shirt
"Please stop it really hurts"
What? Like it hurts when your clothes no longer fit
Or when they say that you wanted it
Or when you try to slit your wrists
Or when they beat you for the hell of it
Or when they say "no, not my man" or "you've got the wrong one"
Or when they say you were having fun
and that you let them bore through one by one by one by one
Or when they look at your beautiful prince and say "he's not my son".

No Womban

Thank you for the word-sound of No Woman No Cry from the dearly departed musical big brother Robert Nestor Marley RIPC (Rest in Peace & Creativity)

"Everything's gonna be alright" R N Marley

Better the devil you know? To that I say Hell No!
When you buck up on a devil; know it's time to go
Know it's time to grow
Time to get to know yourself, love yourself, honour yourself, respect yourself and protect yourself
Time to listen to your inner whisper saying
"Everything's gonna be alright"

Telling people how you fell on the floor.
How you walked into a door
What for? You know your heart's bleeding and you want more
See it's irrelevant, whether or not he says that he loves you
Cos even if he does
You don't need that type of love
Now you know what's next and you know it's time to step
Go on. Turn around and tell me I don't know the rest
How YOU made him vexed and he had a right to sex
It's not his fault that he's stressed
He failed his driving test
And on and on and on
The same ole song
Despite the ins and outs.
This. Is. Wrong.
Implications. Manipulations. Justifications.
Come on sis and change the station
Cos they're not your issues and that is that
You've got your own set of issues and
we done know that
But let him fight his own demons sis
Look at your jaw

Drink bush for your own fever and head for the door

"Everything's gonna be alright"

I hear you call him Your Man. Your Man?
How can you call him Your Man?
When he raises his hand, sis?
That ain't no man
That's a dicktator
A spiritual traitor
Negative instigator
We both know you weren't created for that
Being attacked
Receiving kicks and slaps
Ancestors didn't die for you to live like that
Black eyes and broken bones and now your lips are fat
Ancestors didn't sacrifice for you to live like that

I know you are confused
But listen to your truth
The lies you can refuse but the truth you can't refute

You have a right to choose
So listen to the truth
The truth is abuse
The truth is misuse
Of the power God gave him as a man
Of the power God gave him to stand
Stronger in might than the womb of man
To protect the gift of life
Your death was never part of the plan

Word Sound Volume 1 A Collection of Spoken Word

Hair Peace[9]

*"Many have wept and bled for the kinks in our heads" Hair Peace
That's why I wrote it. No more blood. No more tears*

Narrator:
Come Journey with my hair
Let me take you there
Way beyond your expectations

Encoded in my hair
Our Stories dwell in here
So come on and let me take you there

Ashley had ashy knees
And dry elbows were not her worst disease
But growing up being compared to monkeys swinging on trees
Made a desire straight tresses that would blow in the breeze
But her hair never blew it just stood there
Rain! Sleet! Snow! Wear & tear
To remind her never to fear;
Now over to Shola's colleagues talking 'bout her over there

Colleagues:
"It's so different"
"Is it real?"
"I wonder if she'll let us have a feel?"
"Well I think it's so funky, really, really cool!"
"I know she didn't wear it like that in school"
"Now Shola, a lawyer can't be taken seriously in that 'fro"
"Sort it out. Don't let yourself go"
"Poor thing will it ever grow"

Narrator:
Now here comes Angie…
uh o uh o uh

Angie:
WHAT?!
I don't wanna look like Barbie
But yet everybody thinks I'm barmy
I said I don't wanna be looking like no Posh Spice marga arse barby
But everybody thinks I'm barmy
You wanna know what they wrote about me on the toilet walls?
They wrote my hair is like poo-ber-lic hair[10]
They wrote my hair is like poo-ber-lic hair
Do you know poo-ber-lic hair? You know the type that grows down there ?

But my Mama said, "Do-Do Darling don't wear that frown, Don't let no one make you ashamed to wear your crown, Curls represent the cycle of life that go round and round and round."

Narrator:
This tale is gonna mean a lot to sisters
Weaves, perms and braids giving us mad blisters
Complexes so complex leaving us in a mess as we try to impress not overstanding the depth of our crest
Many have wept and bled for the kinks on our head, being misled and taught that our beauty was dread
So instead of basking in glory we tried to change the story with our hair
To make our lives more fair
(I wonder where), the first sister sat/ who had her naps attacked/ was she slapped or smacked for screaming out like that/ hands tied behind her back/
as misguided elders attempt to buss those naps!
Prior to that did she walk around in a hat?
Headscarf so tight to keep her secret under wraps
Keep it flat/ in case those curls came back to remind her the pain of being Black
Not knowing that Black was beautiful, reflecting fertile soil
Of Merita-Alkebulan-Mama Africa rich in Diamonds, Gold and Oil
And many more minerals, which at points they made her toil
And to justify this they had to spoil her image of self
To accelerate their wealth
In a new world a new girl was born
Away from pride she was torn and scorned made to spawn identity loathing
Now sometimes she suggests it through her clothing,

Sometimes it's revealed through her tears
Sometimes by the path that she has chosen
At other times it's reflected by her hair

Or is it that now times have changed it makes our hair just styles?
Is it just a choice like whether to watch Eastenders or X files?
Is it just random preferences like favouring short or tall guys?
Or about whether or not we perpetrate lies

We are vanguards that's why many follow
Not overstanding the joy and the sorrow
The sleepless nights the plans for tomorrow

See we all have our why's for how we let it flo
Weave, perms, locs or fros
We all have our reasons, some of joy and some of pain, some of pride and some of shame

So Yes
Yes, I am my hair,
Yes, I am my skin,
Full of many great expectations

But I am not just my hair
I am not just my skin,
I'm the mama Africa that dwells within

Word Sound Volume 1 A Collection of Spoken Word

Home

Some place on some day filling in some form. Tick box. British. African. Grenadian. Other

Conditions that seem way beyond repair/ like nobody cares/ so how dare I/ a mere constituent/ attempt to change my reality/ see beyond the banality of my so called existence
Resistance is in my blood line/ since the beginning of time/
let me return/ to a more material line/ so I don't lose you
Though some would argue you're lost already/
True they're not ready/ to come to where you stand and take your hand/ for you've as much to teach as they
Who still pray to false messiahs/ to bring a better day...while waiting to be saved/ 'stead of creating paved roads/ for the children of tomorrow to follow
Sorrow/ plagues my truth within deception/ as I see my global reflection
Of who I am/
AFRIKAN
the dirty word which I'm not supposed to utter/
Forced to say with a stutter/ and an apologetic tone/
To justify why I call Alkebulan. Mama Africa my home

Some say that Africa's not my home
So where's my home?
Is it these streets of London where I roam?
If I was to phone home, where would I phone?
I feel so alone, my mind's blown by seeds that have been sown
For my destruction
Feel free to view this as a construction in imagination
To hide your own frustrations
Of the devastations that we see all around us, but we don't want to discuss
Just cuss and fuss and react instead of act after viewing the facts
The same facts that put the backs up
Of those who call me radical just because I've had enough of this injustice stuff
Dare to call my bluff as it may get rough and cold out here
Can you spare some change?
Can you bear to change?
For inevitable is change
Will it be changes that you make? For the future that you create?

Word Sound Volume 1 A Collection of Spoken Word

UNRESTED SOULS

I 'published' this poem in a sound recording back in 2003. I wrote it after seeing the film Injustice and... I remember sitting in my car outside the community centre[11] and feeling helpless. Powerless. I penned this piece. It saddens my heart that I have to republish this poem. It further tears my heart that I have to republish this poem with the addition of names. Rest in freedom!

I wish that I could do more than just write a poem
Seeing and feeling the injustices I wish that I could just blow 'em away
I mean the inequity makes me wanna start recruiting soldiers
Training them to have a chip on their shoulders
As the system fails us my anger gets bolder
As these cases start to get older and older
Where is the justice as it just gets colder and colder and …?
We must unite and fight for we are right
We mustn't lose sight though the future don't look bright
We must hold on for the light
The light of what? The light of justice
And as I write this verse I think must this
Take a whole lifetime for us to achieve
As those murderers just deceive
As our families and friends grieve
As they break our communities
Spouting technicalities to justify MURDER
Murder: the unlawful killing of one human being by another
Were these not victims of murder? You decide
Break the silence do not hide
Do not let us divide
As the time shall one day come and justice will be done to allow the souls of…

Brian Douglas, Joy Gardener, Shiji Lapite, Ibrihima Sey, Aseta Simms, Wayne Douglas, Orville Blackwood, Roger Sylvester, Christopher Alder, Leon Patterson, Kenneth Severin, Harry Stanley, James Ashley, David Oluwale, Alton Manning, Sarah Thomas, Smilie Culture and all the other brothers and sisters who have been murdered in police custody
To rest as One1

Mark Duggan, Cherry Groce, Michael Brown, Eric Garner, Freddie Gray, Sandra Bland, Kayla Moore, Raynette Turner, Gynnya McMillen, Joyce Curnell, Mzee Mohammed, Tanisha Anderson, George Floyd Rest in Justice

Word Sound Volume 1 A Collection of Spoken Word

BE

I herald this piece as the conscious beginning of my spoken word journey. I thank this poem. I honour this poem. I strive to live this poem.

I used to ask myself why I was here
Living in fear going nowhere
Pretending I didn't care
I used to ask myself how come?
Am I the only one that don't feel right in the United Kingdom?
Sometimes I used to cry ask myself why
Forget it! I'll get high beyond this joint
No matter how hard I tried
The limit stopped at the sky
Life's a lie so what's the point
Though once was the oppressed then became my own oppressor
Rebelled against the system thought that that would make it better
Only to find myself deeper in the game
Not using my brain
Making the same mistakes again and again
Who was I hurting them or me
Not on the plantation yet I didn't feel free
My vision blinkered still I thought I could see
And in my clouded mind I tried to fight reality
I began to walk a very thin line
My head was so far up my butt I thought that I was doing fine
Thought that I was running out of time
Don't know quite when but in a moment I heard the bells chime

"Remove those shackles from your brain
It's ok my dear what you were was temporarily insane
You've not been living your life in vain
You're more than a name, so strip your heart of the guilt and the shame
Remove the chains that bind your soul
Grab a hold release your spirit and let it take control
My child I know you're lost trying to find your role
Look deep inside and your strength will multiply ten fold"

"But what about my hate and what about my anger?
What about my pain and what about my lies?
What about my past I'm scared of tomorrow?"

"Let yourself be filled with natural highs!"

"Why you telling me this? I want it to be easy I do want more but the road's too long
Look I do want to know the truth I don't wanna be inspired
Just bring me back to where I was without my heart feeling wrong"

Bring me back to where I was?
Now that was a joke
Best I tied a rope around my neck and try not to choke
Blindly drifting and definitely broke
Not wanting to acknowledge any spiritual growth
See there was something going on from deep within me
The same that was within my ancestry
The thing that picked my people up the many times they fell
The same thing that let me know I wasn't doing so well
Now the fact that I'm on this planet is a miracle none the less
It truly lets me see that I'm undoubtedly blessed
As I cried out loud somebody heard my song
It didn't take long
They let me know I wasn't wrong
That I could stand up strong and keep going on and on
Bring me back to where I was?
I was brought back to the beginning
Like a foetus in the womb feeling the love that I was bringing
Not thinking about life just simply living
Receiving the protection that my mother was giving
Then I was born unto this world and lovingly embraced
Felt my mother's energy when first she saw my face
Equipped with the tools so I could stand the pace
As my trust misplaced, my energy raped
Treated like a mistake, because of colour and race
How much more could I take? What decisions to make?
What was going on? I was about to break
And now
All I can do is be
The only person I can be is me
Living in full authenticity
Just allowing myself to be free

A Womban's Journey

My eyes were green- but it wasn't from eating vegetables. The world seemed to celebrate my green eyes but my eyes were burning. They were green and covered in bloodshot red. I had to turn them brown. I had to turn them the colour of love. I had to look through my very own eyes, see those eyes staring back at me and love what I saw. One day I did. I really did... and she was born. This is She.

To my dear amazing Sistas
It's been a long time coming so don't think that I've missed ya
To those you walk alone and those who have made unions with our Mista's
This one is for you
You inspire me. Make me who I am
Make me aspire to be the Higher Me
even those who've bun fire pon me
got caught up in jealousy and envy
I forgive thee
cause that thee is sometimes me
when I forget the Miss Story of our greatness
becoming demon possessed
Forgetting that African women have passed every test that humanity has set before us
Khenemet Ankhet
All praises be due
Dear She-Warriors of the Darkest hue
or those blessed with any shade of Black
Never shall I disrespect or attack
Running around calling you words like "ho"
Even if you walk around looking like J-lo,
I simply aspire to inspire growth
To show and let you know that I have travelled back to our wondrous future
So never shall I rebuke ya
I just wanna get to know you better
What I speak of is more than merely gender
I speak of sistahood
Where we forgive the bad and embrace the good
Knowing that we are first
yet for this recognition we often thirst
Our uniqueness labelled a curse
But now no more! As I spread our spirit with verse

Recalling times of when we battled through the worst kind of self-hatred
Dear Queen, Always know that you are not the lowest of the low
know that you are the highest of the high
Whether we look through our first, second or third eyes
As some try with those lies dem a tell
We can tell dem "go to hell"
As they inject hips, lips and batties to induce the swell
Trying to test I and I Nature
As they journey into the land of 'Fake & Faker'
Am I a hater? Nope. I am a lover
Of myself, my sista and mother

Ma Afrika, I your daughter on a mission
to unite her siblings
those who are limping and those who are dribbling
Sending healing so we can stop revealing and selling Big Mama's Blessing
Big Mama, We your girl children, feel your pain
The same way that you've been treated, we been treated the same
Providing the world with sustenance, yet eating late
Being treated worse than dogs and apes
Whilst deep within knowing that this is not our fate
Thus, becoming masters of illusion
Caught in a quagmire of confusion
Told to "Be Black- but not Black Skinned
Be Slim- but not too thin
Stick your butt out and hold your stomach in
Black woman be amazing
Like Grace (or is it Kelly? If you want a man like Nelly)
Don't watch so much telly or you might get a pot belly
Then you'll have to visit the gym for a bout
Doing Kanye's work-out
1, 2, in, out
What did you say? Did you say stressed out?
Sorry I can't hear you you're gonna have to SHOOOUUUUTTTT!!!!
Angry Black woman please calm down
You seem to be heading for a break down!"
NO BREAK DOWN
Just the sound of children saying, "Rise mamas we need you"
so we rise to do what we have to do as the ones who ARE antiquity
Only difference then is when we sat on our thrones we did not sit alone
Forgive me Queens
for I digress
Between studying for big tests
Ensuring food is blessed
Child friendly explanations of sex
So as we do, we do our best

Dear Sista next door,
I feel you as you face interrogation from elders as to "why you ain't have no pickny yet" told that "there's more to life than career and friends"
As you clamp your tongue with teeth so as not to offend

Dear Sista at no. 84,
I know you cannot tolerate more
You don't deserve words like 'sketel' and 'whore'
When you've been served MTV Base since the age of four
Never told to close your legs before
Avoiding fists in kitchens whilst finishing chores
As birds fly across seas and shores

Dear Sistas from Kenya,
Those raped by British Soldiers
For 3 decades and over
After all these years
This government does nothing to heal your tears
I got ya. Anything you need- just holla

To my back in the day girls
forgive me, I was wrong
I never overstood the context whilst we were brukking out to thong song

Bless up Ms Badu, for giving us on and on
'twas there I found endarkenment that kept me holding on

and on and I could go on
Many an issue I could vent
Though I feel this time is better spent letting you know that

I love you
From the first to the last
From the present to the past
Thank you for teaching me and teaching our brothers
in order for us to move forward with each other
as we expand beyond the Babylonian System
Nurturing the womb to bring forth ancestral wisdom
of Kingdom of Queendom of Nation
Ashe

Appendix

1. An adaptation of the article 'Word-Sound' that I wrote for the Reiki Associations Touch Magazine
2. Gil Scott Heron 1949 - 2011 RIPP (Rest in Peace & Poetry)
3. Taken from the documentary Definition of a Poet
4. Wikipedia
5. The same is true for all poems in this collection
6. As performed on BBC Radio's Bespoken Word
7. Reggie Pedro 1972 – 2007 Painter. Artist. Visionary.
8. Angie Stone – Black Brotha
9. Inspired by India Arie's song, I Am Not My Hair
10. She is referring to pubic hair which she mispronounces as poo-ber-lic hair
11. This film was shown in numerous non-traditional film settings as there are some who did not want this film to be shown. These 'some' are supported by the Police Federation who threatened cinemas who screened the film with legal action. This spirit of justice guides this campaign as the film has been screened in over 50 film festivals and received numerous awards.

Endnotes

Destinations for work have included: Africa, USA, other European Countries.

Since the writing of this collection OneNess has been Awarded; Beffta Best Spoken Word Artist, Black Women in the Arts Spoken Word Artist 2014 & 2015 & Women of Substance Spoken Word Award. She has also being sharing her work globally in Africa, The Caribbean, Europe and The USA.

Word Sound Volume 1 A Collection of Spoken Word

Biography

See The World Through New Eyes - Biography By Juanita Rosen Noir

OneNess Sankara's work is her life's passion. From the tender age of eight, she showed an incredible aptitude for the creative arts. Singer, songwriter, lyricist, actress, director and, more recently, musician, OneNess is a vanguard of the arts.

The entire world really is her stage as her work has taken her from Glastonbury to the Royal Festival Hall as well as performances on the BBC, SKY and Choice FM. A further testament to her achievements are the number of accolades she has received including being one of the Top Five Black Female Poets by the New Nation newspaper and the first artist outside of North America to win an award at The Toronto International Poetry Slam. A seasoned performer, she has taken her spoken word to the stage as a solo artist as well as performing as part of the respected poetry quartet, Best Kept Secret. The group's only female member, OneNess compliments her male counterparts with her dynamic performances, the finished product a beautifully unified voice from one of London's most prized spoken word groups.

OneNess adopted her name after it came to her in a particularly vivid dream. This has ultimately changed the course of her life personally and professionally. "Ever since then it's been a journey finding out about OneNess. I've learnt that the name keeps you in check. OneNess is to remind me about the aspiration for OneNess in all aspects of my being." Her chosen surname, Sankara, is an homage to a man who has been described by some as "charismatic and an iconic figure of revolution", a man that OneNess favours for his staunch stance on gender equality. OneNess attributes human nature's ability to withstanding the most trying of circumstances as the fuel that drives her to create 'I have to take things to the next level. I'm very much motivated by the great acts of others. Having to finish a writing assignment or something is minor compared to Harriet Tubman who spent her life helping Africans escape from the plantation. There are people in this world that are in war torn situations, there are people in this country that are homeless, we've all got our stories, but people are surviving through so much that it encourages me to use the talents that I've got".

It is humbling being in the presence of an unassuming artist with a true sense of self and a wicked sense of humour. OneNess is a socially conscious artist with the elevation and education of her community at her heart. To try and label her is to cause your brain to short circuit. She is a connoisseur of art and those exposed to the lyrical workings of Miss Sankara should be fully braced to see the world with new eyes.

Word Sound Volume 1 A Collection of Spoken Word

Thank you for journeying with
me through **Word Sound Vol 1.**

Now I invite you to...
Write your own Word Sound...

www.ingramcontent.com/pod-product-compliance
Lightning Source LLC
Chambersburg PA
CBHW051554010526
44118CB00022B/2708